PRAISE FOR
GIRL AT THE END OF THE WORLD

"In *Girl at the End of the World*, her second, full-length collection published by *Driftwood Press*, one of Erin Carlyle's speakers (an admitted shoplifter) asks, What must it be like / to be an honest girl?" It's a provocative question appearing in a book that with precision and unflinching, clear-eyed honesty explores (among other things) the difficulties of global warming/wildfires, poverty, violence against women, and the loss of a beloved but complicated parent to addiction. Loss and hardship thread through these hard-hitting, spare and beautifully rendered poems, poems that again and again prove the power of language to transform suffering into art."

— Beth Gylys, author of *After My Father: A Book of Odes*

"It's hard / to say if / a crack / in the sky / can ever mend." In this captivating collection, Erin Carlyle confronts the specter of her own girlhood and relationship with her father and his death. Asking questions of origin, belief, memory, and absence, these formally dexterous and inventive poems explore how we see and understand ourselves, and what we may become in the wake of trauma and loss. As the speaker confronts her domestic and ecological environments, she is a "little fish / swimming / back to the beginning." With an unflinching look at personal history and the "ruin" of the past, *Girl at the End of the World* develops a rich, compelling language to dramatize both grief and renewal. Ultimately, the speaker is a woman at the beginning of a new world, with the power to conjure her own future: "What grows after // all trees burn? What will be / born here again?"

— Jennifer Moore, author of *Easy Does It*

"Erin Carlyle's second poetry collection is a temporal triumph, blending the past, present, and future into a heartbreaking and hallucinatory exploration of a girlhood burdened by poverty and the bonds of familial love. These poems bear witness to the ends of many worlds, both public and private: the last kiss of a murdered friend, a community sundered by the opioid crisis, a father's ailing heart, the post-apocalyptic earth. In quiet, luminous lyricism, these elegies teach us about the lonely beauty of survival and dare to ask: 'What grows after / all trees burn? What will be / born here again?'"

— Danielle Cadena Deulen, author of *Desire Museum*

"The world burns down and rises up from the ashes again and again, whether from wildfires, a father's death, 'clocks turning black, / or the dry riverbeds.' And still a girl remains, calling out into the cold cosmos. She is a survivor. Against the advice of grown-ups, she opens a door in the woods and walks through it, entering a place of memory, fantasy, and dream: the realm of poetry. The poems of Erin Carlyle's *Girl at the End of the World* aren't afraid of the dark. They reclaim the magic and power of a time when the wolves in fairy tales lived in the girl's home and around the corner. Carlyle's sharp lines cut, and her stark vignettes will blow you back. Here is the voice of a daughter of so many of our American crises: violence, poverty, climate, opioids. Here is a poet willing to travel to the edge—to outer space, to the room behind the mirror, or to her own darkest memories—and then return to tell the tale."

— Becca Klaver, author of *Ready for the World*

GIRL AT THE END OF THE WORLD
ERIN CARLYLE

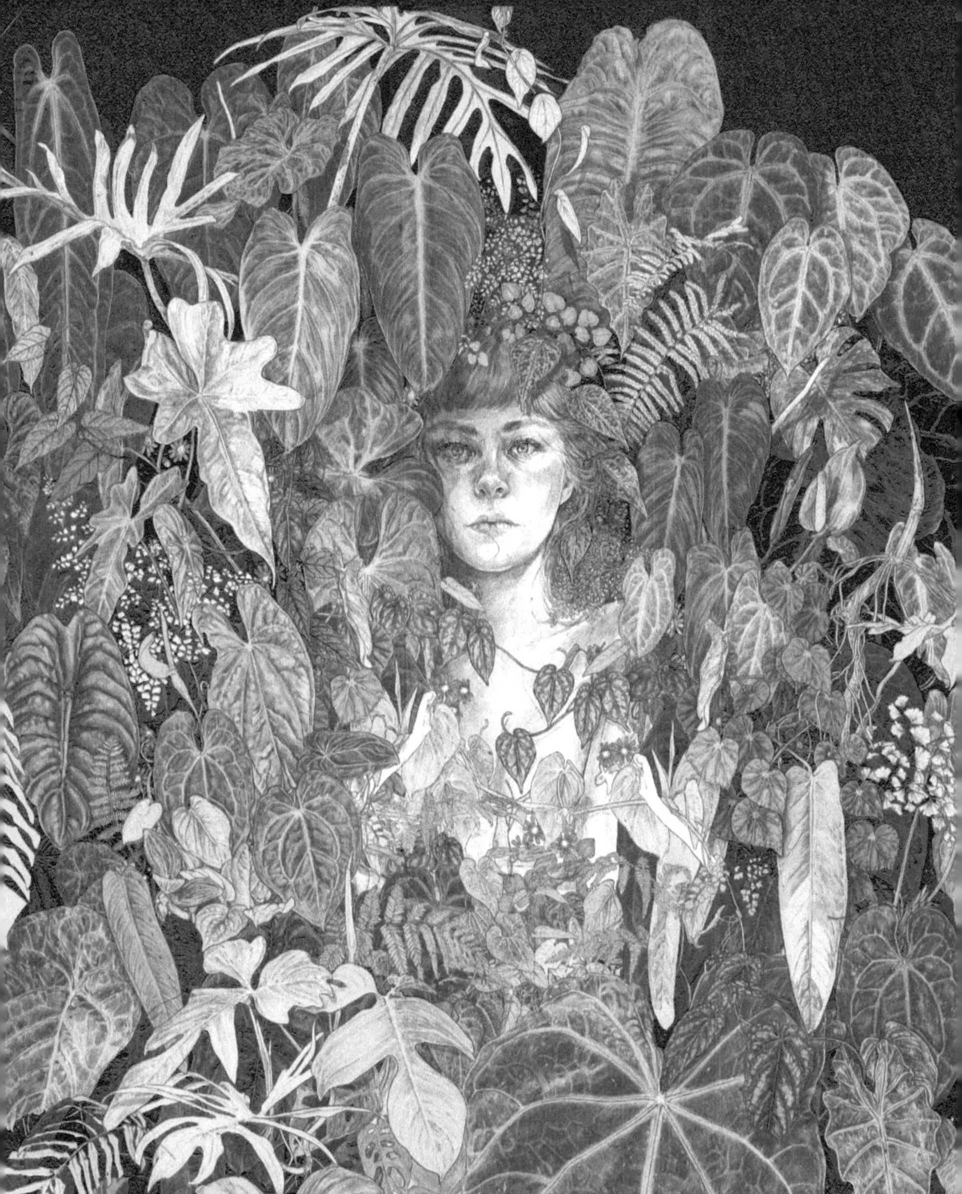

Independently published by *Driftwood Press*
in the United States of America.

Managing Poetry Editor:
Sara Moore Wagner
Cover Design: Sally Franckowiak
Covers & Interior Images: Neva Hosking
Innards Design: James McNulty
Copyeditor: Sara Moore Wagner
Fonts: Rift Soft, Maecenas, Garamond,
& Merriweather

Copyright © 2024 by Erin Carlyle
All Rights Reserved.

No part of this publication
may be reproduced, stored in a retrieval
program, or transmitted, in any form or by
any means (electronic, mechanical,
photographic, recording, etc.), without
the publisher's written permission.

First published on September 17, 2024
ISBN-13: 978-1-949065-33-6
Please visit our website at www.driftwoodpress.com
or email us at editor@driftwoodpress.net.

For Shane, Frank, Sara, and Dorothy

For Daddy and Roger

CONTENTS

I
MY FATHER SIPHONS GAS	3
ARE WE REALLY LIVING IN A SIMULATION?	4
BLACK PEACHES	6
MOON LANDING	7
BABY SIREN	8
TORNADO WARNINGS	9
THE HARD THINGS THAT PULLED US APART	10
DADDY DREAM SUITE	11
OPIOID CRISIS	16
I SAW A NEWS STORY: THREE YOUNG GIRLS, SHOPLIFTERS, CAUGHT	19
A BRIEF HISTORY	20
EVERY HOUSE I LIVED	22
AIRSPACE	24

II
WHAT I READ AS A CHILD	29

III
THINGS WE BELIEVE AS CHILDREN	49
END OF THE WORLD	50
JUST A VILLAGE GIRL	52
TWILIGHT	53
DREAM MAN	54
END OF THE WORLD	55
21 YEARS AGO, IT WAS TODAY	56
THE WHITE ROSES	59
A DREAM AFTER WATCHING *STALKER* DURING FIRE SEASON	60
END OF THE WORLD	61
LOOK INTO A DRESSER MIRROR, DARKLY	62
BELL, BOOK, AND CANDLE	63
TRYING TO COMMUNICATE	64
YES, NO, GOODBYE	66
CAT GUIDE	67
A SPELL	68
END OF THE WORLD	69
TRANSFORMATION	71

INTERVIEW	73

My bones hold a stillness, the far
Fields melt my heart.
They threaten
To let me through to a heaven
Starless and fatherless, a dark water.

— **Sylvia Plath, "Sheep in Fog"**

Everything dies, baby, that's a fact
But maybe everything that dies some day comes back.

— **Bruce Springsteen, "Atlantic City"**

MY FATHER SIPHONS GAS

from a car a few blocks over
from where we're living,

and I am watching him—in our parked car
down at the end of the road.

This is how I see him
in my mind now that I am older,

and he is dead, but I don't know
if the memory was just a dream.

I see myself sitting in the passenger seat
of that old, blue Buick. When he closed

the door behind him, it shook, was louder
than he anticipated—the doors

heavy, metal, and he stopped
for a second, waited to see

if anyone would turn on their porch lights,
but then with a hose tucked

in his arms, he walked on. Was this a dream?
I see myself under a crocheted blanket

in the front seat, careful not to move
or make any more sound,

and my father out there slinking
in the night—poor thief

in search of fuel, and then filling
his mouth with gasoline.

ARE WE REALLY LIVING
IN A SIMULATION?

In the future a computer on the moon runs
        the simulation: Me as a child barefoot
                in the woods, and my momma in her blue

bathrobe cooking ham and beans,
        fried cornbread, and then calling for me
                to come in, eat. Over and over, it repeats my daddy

opening the door of his semi exhausted
        from his haul. He steps down careful
                not to fall, and he never

falls. It replays my daddy calling the police
        on a man in a big car who stopped
                me on the street and tried to get me,

and it repeats me running fast past that little green
        store and my best friend's house all the way home.
                This computer changes the mass

of the moon and its purpose. It'll learn,
        but it's not the same as a lesson
                learned. I don't know if there are people

in this future who smudge
        their foreheads with ash, or people who
                deny themselves food in repentance

except a little bread and water. This is just data
        not ritual: me driving my rental car
                to the funeral home and then claiming

daddy's ashes, and me walking
    through the airport carrying his urn
        in a box. The computer plays

moments, but it can't analyze them, not even
    those moments when my daddy grew stiller
        and stiller. He'll just go and then begin again.

BLACK PEACHES

Flies in the summer

                        don't have to mean death

        like in a still life. Picture
           me as a child riding my Huffy—pink
           and gold, down the middle

of the street. I ride through a cloud of black flies.
     What

                    could they mean?

                Paint this:
                a bowl of peaches, mostly black,

some split, some spilling
their insides out into the bowl,

and a fly already halfway
            through its life.

MOON LANDING

When he went to the moon,
I sat quietly at home, moonless.

I thought to myself: *I'd eat it
all, and the crust of the earth,*

if I wanted to. I don't care
about mapping that cold. I already know

what's there—greyscale, massive. My father
once handed me a map. It had a key

made of little raised markings like broken beer
bottles, but no way to land on the moon.

There was just the impression

of that old county line we'd cross over
and a hint of milkweed in the air.

BABY SIREN

Jump into the deep end.
Feet an arrow to the bottom
of the pool. Vibrations from the summer
children running on pavement,
above me, and then their muffled splashes.
I am a frog swimming back to the top, legs kicking,
awkward spindles. Another girl
jumps in above me,
knocks me back down to the depths
with her tiny legs. I gulp water—mouth
filling. My father must see that I don't arrive
back on the surface as planned—he and his brothers,
drinking Bud, laughing at the motel pool. I try
to swim away from the girl's descent, open eyes burning.
I don't know if she's afraid or if she's trying
to make me afraid, her mouth closing
and opening like the talking doll my dad turned
on in the middle of the night to scare me—head rotating
back and forth. This girl is trying
to communicate, but it comes out in bubbles
and bursts, almost soundless. I swim up, but she grabs
my legs, pulls me back down. She wants
me to grow fins—be with her, mermaids
forever, but I don't want to stay
here. My father must feel me struggling
to stay human, must see the sound rise in waves
on the surface. The girl climbs up my body,
arms around me—hugs that pull me down,
but before she has all of me,
I force my arms out wide, breaking her embrace
no longer her prisoner,
and when I rise to light, finally head above
the water, I see my father is nowhere.

TORNADO WARNINGS

i
First, Daddy stared me in the face
and said *I'm not scared*

of a little wind and water
as we turned to watch the violence

in the trees outside. I could see
thrill in his eyes, and I gripped

the front door, hid my little body
behind—head peeking out. I kept saying

come inside until he finally
did just before a branch crashed
down in the yard.

ii
Daddy tells us all to go
in the bathroom, and then he goes
outside to watch the sky swirl. Danger

is a sudden pressure
change in the room. We can't afford

a basement, so we gather
in and around the tub.

He comes back,
circles his arms around us—a shield.
This happens once a year, or twice

when the moon is covered with dark clouds,
and the hot and cold air mix.

We wait it out every time.
We never die.

THE HARD THINGS THAT PULLED US APART

I'm listening to the album *Nebraska* and in the second to last song, Springsteen dreams he runs to his father's house only to find someone else living there. It makes me think of my dad who never owned a house, and that I could never run to any of the houses where we used to live, but sometimes I do dream of the blue shotgun house we lived in when I was eight. The windows were so large, and I was scared there could be another bad world behind the heavy curtains left over from the last tenant. Momma made me brush them with a damp cloth to keep the dust away, and I stayed up all night in my room that doubled as the dining room, watching to make sure the devil didn't come through.

DADDY DREAM SUITE

He sends me

a spirit: black dog,

        skin and bones. The dog

says: *It's hard*

to say if   *a crack*   *in the sky*

    can ever mend.   I only half

understand, and then the dog asks

    me if I ever knew

the difference between   the tone

    of the crystal

    versus the glass bowls

    that used to live

in my grandmother's hutch.

    I nod, but it's a lie.

The spirit gives me

    instructions

    anyway, and though I am

>   not ready to guide
>
> daddy   out of his grave,
>
> I put my hand
>
>   in the softened earth,
>
> and pull him out
>
>   headfirst, born
>
>   for the second time.
>
> I take him
>
>   to a diner, get him
>
> eggs and toast, and he   shimmers
>
>   before me
> in and out of existence.

* *

        He shimmers in

and out   of existence,

                and the trees

around the diner

        are burning. Birds drop

    outside the window, dead.   Orange sky

and orange juice

        for breakfast.

When Daddy is

        where I am,

he tells me   the names of all the dogs

        that, as a child,

        he buried

in his back yard—old

    regrets,   and when he goes

    to the other side,   I hear

        nothing.

* *

The air

    is bad here, but still,

        we exist   past August

and September   before

    he's gone   completely—the trees

are all burned too,

    some into ashen

        stumps and some

into black forms

        of their old selves. I get

up from the table, pay the bill.

* *

      I pay the bill and look

at our table. Daddy hasn't come

      back to this place,   he's gone

somewhere— absent of light   or somewhere

            he can manifest

as dark, hot hands reaching out.

      All the people   in the diner talk

about are the fires: trees

           burning—cremations,

     ash   falling into the river,

      and when they use   the word deceased,

it feels better

      than hearing *dead or they're dead, they died*

      or *he died, he's dead.*

OPIOID CRISIS

I am just like the people

who came before   me—water-wrinkled

out of the green

mucky creek. From that watery hole,

we rose—our teeth

already dark,

cavitied. No one gave

us a penny to rub

rub—or a job to make

any, and then my daddy died

for twelve hours—foam

on his lips

like that green creek. I have never

gotten over it.

He dug holes in the land

and he

hauled goods long distances

until his heart gave out.

The doctor pulled it out of his chest

and he couldn't do anything

anymore,

had to

take pills from orange bottles

but had no coins

to survive   and then he died

from the pills and I buried him

in a different hole

in the ground, but I wanted

to go

again to the old

water—little fish   swimming

back to the beginning,

emerge human

and grab

grab my mother and brothers,

and daddy, and pull them out to the cold earth

to the start of our lives

again

before he died

and we all had more

than twelve hours left

to foam, but no coins

no coins

in our pockets.

Nothing, only pills

to buy

the dirt, the ground.

I SAW A NEWS STORY: THREE YOUNG GIRLS, SHOPLIFTERS, CAUGHT.

Wanting is not a crime. At sixteen, I would steal
anything I could
—eyeliner, candy, homework,
boyfriends. Once, I helped steal
a toilet from a construction site,
and I kissed a boy I didn't know
that night. Who knows who
he belonged to? I owned nothing. Even my shoes
came from my best friend's closet.
At least I come by stealing honestly. My father
took things from the neighbors'
yards to sell. He took
gas from their cars, even took
money from my grandmother's purse. Stealing
is my birthright. When I was a teen,
I downloaded a credit card
generator, typed in the numbers of each card
until one of them worked. I bought clothes,
CDs, and once I bought a few cans of duck
meat because I had never
tried it before (too oily). Even now,
I'm eying my neighbor's dog—alone
on their porch all day,
and I have to remind myself
that I can buy
what I don't have already.
What must it be like
to be an honest girl?

A BRIEF HISTORY

of the Woods

I am in a dark soft hole.
My mother put me here.
I smell of white

cream. My mother lies
on the ground near me.

of Moons and Stars

It's on the tip of my tongue,
your new name.
Daddy, you exchanged me

for another daughter-formed
constellation and you passed moons
bigger than a family.

Of dogs and other animals

"All dogs die," he said.
Flattened out on the road,

or poisoned by chocolate.

Of sickness

Vulnerable skin cut down
and across. They peeled you.

I sat on the opposite side

of the room trying to understand
how I could look just like you.

I crossed my eyes, squinted,
and got ready to leave you.

Of home

I've seen a tree shed its skin
and swarms of red-winged

black birds in the wetlands
and around creek beds. I've pulled

leaves off a branch to form
a fleeting flower. I've wished

for my puppy to come back to life.

Of travelling

I slid down the dirt hill
looking for the river. Later

I fell asleep curled up—little
pillbug. Then you picked

me up and put me to bed.

EVERY HOUSE I LIVED

Inside paint flakes
and drywall cracks.

I sit cross-legged in a room
reading a *Seventeen* magazine,

candles on the floor,
wax dripping. In the corner,

my younger girlself floats, surrounded
by other twelve-year-old girls—*light
as a feather.*

The house creaks and moans.
In the hall

my mother collapses
in seizure—too many pills,

and shirtless Daddy sits in the living
room baring his deep chest, heart scar.

I cry on the couch—dropped
the tea jug, got a spanking.

All the dirty dishes
soak in soapy water in the kitchen sink,

and Momma and Daddy sleep
on their double bed, sun

coming in their bedroom windows.

I hear *Dark Side*
of the Moon,

and my brother is miming drums
while girl-me watches, quiet.

Outside, the house shimmers,

and we hear that old tornado
we all hid from. It rumbles.

AIRSPACE

Ghosts sit watching planes
lifting—liminal space. A long time ago

my dad took my brother and I to an airport

just to ride the shuttle from one
end to the other. We watched

people board their flights,
and then we watched other people claim

baggage from the carousel. My dad—fresh

shaved, in his thirties, grabbed my face
in his hands, so excited

to teach me about traveling
somewhere else only to come back home.

WHAT I READ AS A CHILD

Once when I was 9, I read a book
about a hard girl who didn't believe
in anything, not even stars. She was

sure those things in the night
were dots colored in by someone
very tall.

* *

By some miracle
or accident, the girl became
a ghost.

This was a strange book
with a tall tree in the middle,
but the girl

had no one to talk to.
A ghost alone in grief.

* *

When my father died, I thought of that book,
and I thought about a dream.

* *

I opened a door
                    I found
in the woods, walked through
it. My mother said never go through
a door you don't know.

* *

On the other side
of the door, I heard my dad,
but when I opened this door,
all I saw was a clearing
with just one
tall, skinny pine tree in the middle.

* *

Now I'm thinking about another book.
This one about a mouse.

Her husband died,
and she had to find
a way to take care of her kids,
                          so she went
on a journey.
She met a lot of mice
        along the way. I know

each one had a special name.

I have to say, I was a quiet child.
I always had my head
in a book.

* *

And I miss
my dad's blue Buick. And I miss reading
in the backseat.

* *

And I missed the pine-
tree lined highway
because I was reading.
My father let me ride in the front seat.
My father let me ride in the front
My father let me ride in the
My father let me ride in   .
My father let me ride
My father let me
My father let
My father

* *

I walked through the door to see the lonely
pine tree, and I couldn't
tell how old it was.
Even a young
pine grows tall.

* *

When I wanted to leave the clearing, I turned
to find the door, but it was gone.
I looked

and looked. It was cold.

* *

I also read a book about time
travel. I'm trying
to remember the cover design.

I'm trying to remember.

* *

After a long time with no door,

I sat on the ground,
and ran my hand through the grey
dirt. I cried out
for my father. I cried.

I could still hear him.

* *

Now that I'm thinking about it, there was a book about a golden thread.

* *

When I think about that thread,

I think about
all the books my father burned
in his life—buried
the remains under our old trailer's porch.

How is this the world?

* *

I closed my eyes,
and I must have fallen asleep because when I opened them again,

                              I was finally home, fatherless.

* *

Once upon a time.
That's how another book started.
Once upon
a time, there was a girl and that's all
                                        that I remember.

THINGS WE BELIEVE AS CHILDREN

I thought that if I believed in God,
I would end up a child bride

for David Koresh. I dreamed
King David told me: *the firmament*

lives between your soft, skinny thighs,

and I asked him for the difference
between life and death,

or if someone would eventually burn
down a compound with my children

inside. I asked him,
what if I fall into a grave with no bell

tied around my toe? What if I get
to the underworld as an overripe fruit?

He looked at me through those golden
wire-rimmed glasses and asked me:

do you want to be a ghost?

END OF THE WORLD

I'm sitting at a bus stop, waiting
to get a lift

to some other plane
of existence.

The trees in this town
used to sway, almost whisper.

Now they're too dry,
some dead, but I have a memory

of kissing a boy
under these oaks.

Clean, pastoral, we laid

down on the cool, soft earth,
and the earth was spongy, gave

under the weight of our bodies.
I know that there were other

trees here too:
Pine, White Ash, Silver

Maple, American Beech,
and it smelled old,

like dirt, the body
of the earth. The boy slid his hand

under my shirt and I sucked
in the air, filled

my lungs—fresh, but I stopped him
before heavy breathing,

made my hand
guide his hand

out into the crisp light
of day. I told him

it was too fast. I didn't get
a second date, never saw him again.

Now, I'm sitting here looking
at the burn and ruin trying

to breathe like that,
but it's too hard.

I want to give
up, and I don't think

there's a bus coming,
but there is a bird circling above.

JUST A VILLAGE GIRL

He tells me he'll eat me
up as we cross over
the wooden bridge. The air

here is thick. It clings. My father
never told me about the wolf

in the woods, or that
that wolf might put me in a bag
and throw me over its shoulder. In my heart,

he never locked one single window, my father,
so when the wolf asked me
for a walk, I left

everything behind, and when he said dark,
strange things, I thought: *he's just a stupid wolf,*

but then the moon got full,
and I realized I left
without shoes. And when the wolf

got inside my belly, I knew I had to choose:
digest him or birth him back out.

TWILIGHT

Think about her
when she was still alive,

how she lined her eyes with electric blue
eyeliner, went to a party

where boys who drive their dads'
new cars kept trying to make her

laugh with dirty jokes, kept
trying to touch her long arms.

She was horrible in her beauty, thin wrists,
skinny fairy queen. I wanted

to be like her—body shimmering
there in the dark of the room.

And then she walked to me, kissed me
just before she got into a car

with a guy. I stood there for a minute,
and then I fixed my mouth

in a mirror
before I left the party.

DREAM MAN
FOR POLLY KLAAS

My father said I can't do it—fall
asleep with my window open.

He would tuck me in, leave
a light on, walk back down

the hall—a smoke trail.

When I was close to Polly's
age—a year apart, I was afraid

to think about her slumber
party. A man pulled her

from the thickness
of her dreams, tied her hands,

told her friends to count
to a thousand—their heads in pillow

cases. He said: *I only want her.*

I told my father this story,
and he said:

men will do what men will do.

END OF THE WORLD

I am a girl at the end
of the world. Did I hear

about clocks turning black,

or the dry riverbeds
before now? No, I didn't.

I ate then slept each day.
I repeated. Did I see the green

vines browning—crackle
then disintegrate on the ground? No, I did not,

but now that it's too late, I see,

and all I can do
is climb this wall without gloves,

and on top of this old bank,
I'll look out at the destruction.

While I'm up here, I am going to pull out
my hair, lose the ability to read.

When I come back down
again, I'll just rake that dusty land

with my fingers and forget
to start the whole world back

again. Now that I think about it:
did I hear about the hole in the sky?

21 YEARS AGO, IT WAS TODAY

In the past, we saw stars form
out of a vast black, and it became

a swirling glittering nebula.
I remember that at the time we thought

all the girls who came
before us here in the woods, flashed

in the pink spiral of the sky—big bang,
propelling forward, the future.

In the past, we were two girls
walking together, picking up rocks,

putting them in our pockets—little
weights. We traveled

down to the green creek smoking clove
cigarettes, discussing tarot and divining.

Now that we are finally
in the future, will we be able to hold

hands at the edge of this black
hole—event horizon, and if we go

in, will we come
out somewhere else? I don't understand.

* *

In the absence of light, we are

        girls   again

We are girls

           only

when it's

      dark.

THE WHITE ROSES

One spring, at one of my parent's rented
houses, I looked across

the street at a white rose
bush, noticed many of the roses bloomed early,

had started their wilt
but still some were new, full, shock of white. I noticed

that after it rained,
the petals held the rain drops

for just a short time as the Southern sun,
already so hot, dried up everything

around. In our yard, there was also a bush—big,
green, no flowers. After school, in a childhood act

of cruelty, I'd stash candy wrappers and Coke cans
in its dense leaves, and when I found

a porno magazine in my father's sock drawer,
I looked at the naked women, their breasts

full—tear drops, and I tore it up,
stashed it in the bush with my other

trash. No one ever asked me about it,
and if my father noticed, he didn't say anything.

A DREAM AFTER WATCHING *STALKER* DURING FIRE SEASON

The Stalker brought us here
to speak to a telephone—a landline

in a toxic room. The landscape here
was changed by some long dead

company who never took
the blame, and before we can

use the phone, we must pass through
a corridor made of sand.

This journey makes me think:
How is sand made into glass?

The Stalker says we'll have to tell
our secrets, and once he hears

ours, he'll spill
his too. He brings us

to a barren land, but he knows
each little change in the landscape,

and though change can feel
like witchcraft, he makes us

hold onto science
by recording

each waving, little, dry
piece of grass—camera in hand.

END OF THE WORLD

If I stop to look at the stars,
they'll catch me—men with guns.

They threaten to rape and kill
any woman travelling

after dark.
I used to think the movies

were wrong about how fast
people return to violence,

but there must be a cannibal
reaction buried deep

inside us,
and when the power goes out,

eating begins. When I was a child,
I believed in witchcraft—female

power in the snap
of a finger.

I try so hard to call
on that power. I snap

my fingers, but I only hear
the crack of dead branches.

LOOK INTO A DRESSER MIRROR, DARKLY

In my old teenage bedroom, I'd sit
drawing words with my finger
in the air

and then I'd try to send
those messages though my dirty
dresser mirror to the other side.

I'd write: *Who
is there? Do you want
anything? What can I do?*

And I'd get nothing.
This was before I had a cellphone,
before quick connection. Alone

for hours, I'd try to reach
through. I'd stare at the glass and imagine
my face turning
into someone else's face,

my round cheeks switching
to long, gaunt—practical effects,
a horror show, skin peeling

revealing more skin. Though I begged
for a word, this new girl would never
speak to me or tell me anything.

She'd watch
as our face stretched, uncanny,
almost real.

BELL, BOOK, AND CANDLE

A girl walks toward me dressed
in red. Look

at the open field
where we sit.

We put our hands to the ground
then touch our bodies, blood runs

down my leg. My mother
is watching from behind a tree,

water running down her leg. The girl
pulls out a candle, a leather-bound book,

and a brass bell. I hear my father
or a dog somewhere behind us,

and when I look back at the old tree
—my mother is gone.

I am blood-soaked, ruined
panties, but never have I ever

felt ecstasy like this before. I join
their hands and feel my life flash.

TRYING TO COMMUNICATE

In my dreams,
wolves talk to me

as they turn
into other wolves.

Before my eyes,
they slip their skin off,

change form.

  *

It feels like a hundred years
since I spoke to you

on the phone.
I remember the crack

of the line, and your
voice: *goodbye*.

  *

I heard that bees
whisper messages

in a chain,
so the dead might

feel like they're still alive.
I speak to any bee I see.

*

And I go into the water
at night looking
for the other end

of the string

that used to run from
my body to your body.

*

In my dream, there is always
one wolf who becomes

my mother and one wolf
who becomes my father.

YES, NO, GOODBYE

The planchette begins to move
on its own, but I stop it
with my right hand. I say:

*is this someone
coming through?*
The planchette answers yes
or no questions, misspells words. I ask
the basics: *are you okay, did it hurt,*

are you happy? Each time
it moves, I want to feel
pressure, a hand on my hand,

but what I feel is an itch,
and an urge to pull away. I ask:
what do I do now,

and the planchette moves
fast—wild motion.

I ask: *what are you now?*

CAT GUIDE

People say cats can

speak with the dead, and you know

it's true. We've all seen a cat

communing with a spirit in the corner

of the room, ears pointed forward,

puffed tail. When my grandmother died,

all I had around were

my uncle's dogs bumping my hand

for pets, lying at my feet,

following me to bed—loving companions,

but when my father died,

my cat ran around my apartment,

mad, full of my grief, wailing, possessed,

and then suddenly she stopped cold, and I caught her

looking up at the ceiling, expectant, waiting.

A SPELL

Drop a jug
of tea on the floor,
shatter it.

Ask your momma
for forgiveness.

Cut a green switch.
Stand still, take the blow.

Ask your momma
how to talk
to the dead.

Sit on the couch,
frozen, watching
the screen door hook and eye

rattle with the wind.
Watch it unlatch.

END OF THE WORLD

A ghost lives
in a fake haunted house.
He watches

jump scares, enjoys
the wire pully system
that opens the doors and cabinets

all while visitors walk
around in semi-darkness, laughing
with gleeful fear.

He hears people repeat
legends: *witch, soldier, child, plague,*
but he never participates.

He is a short-range
wanderer floating around,
observing—taking note,

doing nothing else, and only
one woman in all the time

of his death spotted him
just in the corner of her eye.

Now, it's the end of the world,
and he's surprised
he feels so alive.

He looks out the attic window, sees
a dark red flash in the sky, hears

a sound like a burlap sack ripping,
and for a split second

he wonders:
What grows after

*all trees burn? What will be
born here again?*

TRANSFORMATION

Before my dad's funeral, I watched

my mom fumble in the trash for a Xanax

she dropped. I helped her find it

buried deep at the bottom under coffee grounds

and other discarded things.

By the smell, the trash hadn't been

taken out since he died. I sifted through the stuff

he threw away, still rotting there

though it had been a week: fruit, food wrappers,

cigarette butts, old meat. He was gone, but the trash

was still there, breeding life, something

from something else. I found her pill

under it all, and I handed it to her

with a glass of water.

BETWEEN TENDERNESS & DANGER
A CONVERSATION WITH ERIN CARLYLE & SARA MOORE WAGNER

Erin, I am so excited to publish your second *Driftwood Press* book. Your first, *Magnolia Canopy Otherworld*, was a big reason I also sent work here. Your voice and craft are strong and really capture the *Driftwood* aesthetic. I'd love to hear about the way these books connect for you. What is the relationship of *Girl at the End of the World* to *Magnolia Canopy Otherworld*? Where do you see them intersecting and diverging?

    Thank you! I am so very excited for you all to publish my second full-length collection. *Driftwood* has been amazing and supportive to my work, and I appreciate it beyond words. *MCO* was a work of autobiography, in a way. It was like the first books of so many poets who have written before me—a purging of my childhood. It was also a book that contemplated girlhood and how we are shaped by the place we come from and the things we witness as children. I do carry some of that into this new book in that I am still working with memory. I started writing this book after my father died from an overdose as a result of his 30+ year addiction to opioids. While this book does deal with the opioid crisis much like I did in *MCO*, it's more an exploration of memory and death. The first section is a lot about my dad, and then in the second section, there is a long poem that is kind of descent into an underworld of grief. The third section comes out into magical thinking, but the speakers are also surrounded by dangers to their minds and bodies, fires, and visions of the end of the world.

    As I was writing the early poems in this collection, we were in the scariest times of the pandemic, before the vaccine. I lived in California, in my husband's hometown, and I was experiencing my first real "Fire Season." In the book, my poems are conflating the death of my father with the death of the trees and wildlife during this time.

It's interesting that you were away from home while writing this. The feeling of "home" is so immediate. Are you like James Joyce in that you write better with distance from place? What is it about being away that often brings these places closer?

    I have been away from the places I call home (Kentucky and Alabama) for a long time now, but I always have such a vivid imagination of these places that comes through in my work. Being away from home has given me a perspective distance that helps me to interrogate those spaces. Because I don't have a strong connection to my family, largely due to how opioids affect everyone (it's complex), I don't visit home often. Home is mostly in my head, I guess.

The idea of home being just in your head is so fascinating to me! You create atmosphere and place in a poem so well. From your first poem, we are drawn into the landscape of your speaker's childhood. How important do you think establishing place is in poetry? Are there poets you turn to who also do this exceptionally well?

I am really rooted in the places I grew up. I think about them often maybe because I moved around so much, so I try to add it all up to something like a childhood home. I just think that the place you start in keeps its hold on you forever. These places always find their way into my work.

Many of my favorite poets do this as well. Cynthia Cruz writes about California, and in many of the poems in Diane Seuss's *Frank: Sonnets*, you get glimpses of the town she grew up in.

I'm also thinking about first poems structurally. Your first poems set up the argument of the book, introducing place and the major tone, characters, and conflicts. How do you go about ordering a collection? What do you think is the function of those first poems in any book of poems? Were there any collections you looked to to model this that you might recommend?

Putting things in order is not my strong suit in my non-poet life. I am not an organized person. It does not come easily to me. Putting together a poetry manuscript is just as hard. When I'm writing, I know there is a kind of story going on, but what comes first, second, third is a puzzle. I'm stuck on the magic of the number three (even though I'm not a magical thinker). It feels stable and easily creates a book arch when you work in threes, so I stuck with three sections again for this book.

I was inspired by poets like Karyna McGlynn in her book *I Have to Go Back to 1994* and *Kill a Girl*. The first poem in her book informs the feeling of the rest of the book, and the story of the collection unfolds in three sections: Planchette, Visitant, and Revenant. If you haven't read that book, you really should!

So much like McGlynn, the first poem in my collection sets up the rest of the book. In this poem it could be a dream, or it could be something her father really did. It sets up the mystery and danger of her father. For me this poem informs the rest of the section, but also sets up the feelings in the rest of the book.

These poems move so well between danger and safety, sometimes holding us in that dual space at the same time. This feels so much like that fragile state of childhood, especially girlhood. How do you build and maintain that tension in your images?

I'd like to think that not everyone had a childhood where they had these conflicting feelings, but I'm sure there are lots of people whose identities make it impossible to fully enjoy a moment. You could be swinging on a swing set at the park, smelling the wind as you pick up speed, and you get a tingling feeling that you should look behind you just in case. I am working with those feelings in my work.

For instance, the girl in the first poem is sitting in her family's car under a crocheted blanket while her father is slinking around in the night looking for cars to siphon gas from. There is a familiarity with a blanket like this that your grandma or aunt makes, but it's out of place in such a dangerous scene. The father cares enough to tuck her in, but he puts her in danger by leaving her alone to do his work. There is always a push and pull between tenderness and danger in my work. These moments are not cut and dry. This father is not wholly good, and the place where this girl lives is beautiful, but can be hostile at times.

Your work almost feels Southern Gothic, at times, in the looming danger in the rural spaces, and that hint of the supernatural. Are you a fan of Southern Gothic? Is there something about the South that lends itself to this kind of atmospheric horror? Is this something you were thinking about when writing these poems?

Yes! I am a big fan of horror in general, and I am from the South and grew up with lots of ghost stories and folk tales. When I was a kid in Kentucky, there wasn't a corn field that didn't have some evil people doing witchcraft or some other dark magic in the rows, at least according to the local kids. I am not a magical thinker, I trust the scientific method and am not religious, but I do still hold all those tales dear, and they do make their way into my work.

Horror and the Gothic have always been genres where artists can explore grief. I'm thinking of more art-house films like *Midsommer* by Ari Astor or even going back to an American Gothic creator,

Poe. Both authors explore the horrific parts of grief. My work isn't as scary as these two examples, but I do work in this vein.

As far as Southern Gothic is concerned, yes! The South is both uniquely beautiful and horrifying. Obviously, it's important to keep in mind the specific ways the legacy of Slavery has shaped the South when thinking about its ghosts and legends, but also there is a mask and reality situation going on here. On the one hand, there is the presentation of The South as environmentally rich, architecturally beautiful, and culturally polite, but on the other hand, there are the historical oppressions that influence what happens behind closed doors.

Your Sylvia Plath epigraph has me thinking about Plath's relationship to her father. In the recent *Red Comet: The Short and Blazing life of Sylvia Plath***, Heather Clark explores Sylvia's relationship with her father Otto Plath, her early idealizing, then eventual deconstruction of in poems like "Daddy," where the Daddy figure both is and isn't Otto. Perhaps it's all our jobs, as daughters and as poets, to reconsider what we inherit from our fathers on a literal and metaphoric level. How closely did you keep to the character of your actual father? "Daddy Dream Suite" feels very Plath-esque to me! How much did Plath's approach influence you?**

I have been studying for my PhD comprehensive exams, and one of the requirements is to compile a list of 30 contemporary books centered around a theme of our choice. I am thinking about the legacy of Confessionalism on the way poets today write the personal. In my reading, I have noticed that a lot of women and queer poets have a connection to Plath (and Sexton) in that they actively quote her work, comment on it, or even just mention their love for her. There are some things that we see as problematic in her poems today, but that initial reading and connection to her rawness is something that has shaped a lot of poets, myself included.

My dad has been a central figure in my art and poetry for my whole life. Much like Plath, his life and then eventual death weigh on me, which is why I picked that quote for the beginning of the book. The daddy in my poems is like a worry stone being worked over and over, but it's all from my perspective or from stories I heard. I don't know him really. In "Daddy Dream Suite", I am really conflating the death of the land in California with my dad's death. It's not really him in the poems. It's just the grief of him. It's grieving him while I could literally smell smoke in the air from the fires raging all around Sacramento.

Tell me more about this "legacy of Confessionalism." Where do you see this book fitting into that? How do you feel about those who use "confessional" as an insult?

What I mean by that is simply what people felt they were able to write about after the confessional movement. There have been poets who write about their lives before, and there were many writers of color, poets in the Black Arts Movement (like Nikki Giovanni) for instance, who were writing about their experiences at the time as well, so I don't want to just contribute writing about "the personal" to The Confessional Poets who were mostly white writers. All these poets had an impact on how poets write today and how we see the lyric "I." The confessional movement was not filtered through mythology or allusion as in the past. A lot of poets in that movement—Sylvia Plath, Anne Sexton, and Robert Lowell come to mind—resisted formalist constraints by conveying their rawest emotions in their poetry. I write about my life and the people and places that I have encountered and events that shaped me. I don't think I am confessing (and if I'm correct, I don't know that many of the confessional poets liked this title or felt they were at confession as if in a Catholic church), but I am digging into myself to bring out some kind of truth or some kind of story that connects to other people or a larger social issue. The "I" in my work isn't always just me. It's sometimes me, but other times it's a mixture of people. It's sometimes just a feeling that I've turned into an "I."

As far as using confessional as an insult, anytime something is deeply personal, people feel uncomfortable about it. I am a big Tori Amos fan, and I remember that when she came out the press called her a "confessional singer/songwriter." To me, this diminished what she did, which was an exploration of being a young woman at that time, and fans understood that connection. I remember back then some guy asked me what my favorite band was, and I said Tori Amos, and he said, "she's good, but her music is kind of solipsistic." He had turned her interrogation of her experience into a variation on a familiar refrain—she's too subjective, she just whining, and she just likes to write about herself. This is usually a quick way of dismissing those experiences as irrelevant. I am also a big Sharon Olds fan, and I have been in graduate classes where people have had similar issues with her work and have called her work solipsistic or confessional.

I will say that the term doesn't really describe what poets are doing when they are sharing personal moments from their lives. It isn't religious for me. It is some form of connection, but it's not just a trauma dump.

I completely agree, and I share your love of both Tori Amos and Sharon Olds! I can see some of their and Plath's influence in the way you approach the sometimes taboo subject of addiction, how you approach the opioid crisis, something we both explore in our poems. There is a real tendency to vilify or other the addict, especially the poor or marginalized addict. It can also start to look like poverty-porn, if not done right. You have such a light and empathetic touch here. What advice do you have for others who might want to approach taboo subjects like this in their poems?

I have nothing but empathy for people affected by addiction and especially those affected by the opioid crisis because I have seen firsthand just how easy it eats away at a life. It can be nice at first and slow, but it eventually takes ahold of everything. I also saw the way that some people treated my father, especially those in law enforcement and other positions of power over him. He started out as a person and ended as an addict. I have a lot of personal anger towards him, but that doesn't negate what he had to endure for so many years.

If you are writing about a subject like this, you can't sit only in your anger because ultimately, not everything is about you. When I write about my dad or anyone in my family, I try to remember their humanity. It's not always easy.

In section two, you have the long poem "What I Read as a Child" which not only breaks up the book structurally but explores the narratives which create the landscape of girlhood. As someone who loves folklore and fairy tales, I was wowed by this. I am also in awe of how profoundly, in its simple lines, it captures the unexplainable grief of losing a parent, the struggle to remember and make sense of so many things. Tell us more about the genesis and form of this long poem.

Sometimes I just sit down and see what comes out. I write kind of organically in that I may have an impression of what I want to say, and then I just see what happens. This poem was a bit differently formed. It existed in my head for a long time, and I knew exactly what I wanted to do. I knew the structure, and I knew that it would explore a dream sequence that explored my grief, and that it would jump around from that to impressions of books I read as a child. Reading has always been an escape for me, especially when I was younger. I see the poem as a journey through an underworld of sorts.

I also liked the idea of one poem taking up an entire section of the book. I like when other poets do this as well. I'm thinking of Jennifer Moore's book *The Veronica Maneuver*.

Fairy tales have always been important to me. These were some of my earliest means of escape. There is also a reference to *Mrs. Frisby and the Rats of Nimh* in this poem. Not sure if anyone remembers that book. It was very formative for me! Reading and stories have been one of the great loves of my life.

The end of the book turns towards space, that expanse of sky, in a way that reminds me somewhat of Tracy K. Smith's *Life on Mars* **in which she too turns to space, science fiction, and the infinite to reckon with the loss of her father. In your book, this look at the universe feels also charged with witchy, feminine energy. What is it about grief that pulls our faces upward? How do you see this draw to the cosmos functioning in your collection?**

I love that book so much! This book started because I didn't know how to consider my dad dead. It was weird to me that he was talking to me on the phone a week or so before he died, and then he was just gone. I don't believe in religion, so I didn't have that to fall back on. I do believe in energy in that we consume food to make energy to stay alive, and that all matter cannot be destroyed. Matter is just turned into some other thing or used to make something else. That was comforting, but then it wasn't like HE was out there, just the matter that made him up was somewhere. I started to kind of have magical thinking about the universe. I thought about other universes where maybe he didn't get addicted to opioids, or where we didn't have a strained relationship. I thought about time travel. I watched sci-fi and read sci-fi. Then, I started to venture from that to thinking about when I was a teenager, when I did think magic was real, a time when I played around with the tarot and thought about being a witch. Both of these fantasies conjured the dead. They were both a way for me to escape into thinking about a reconciliation with my dad. Maybe it's just natural to want to figure death out. Maybe it's just part of the process.

In the end, the book doesn't hold humans above the natural life cycle, which is why I brought in Fire Season. We all die, and we then transform into something very organic and able to die again. It's not a bad thing.

I am wondering about the role of the mother in this collection. She is "the other wolf," and water, not blood, runs down her leg in "Bell, Book, and Candle." The book ends with the

mother taking a Xanax. **What does this final choice mean for you, for your speaker, for all of us as girls in a now fatherless world? Could this, in a way, be the end of the world?**

I wanted to end with a relationship between women. The last section has a lot of poems that center around the dangers of being a woman. I didn't want to idealize my father or fathers or patriarchy. This isn't a book about a good daddy who died. This is a world where mothers and daughters pick up the pieces of the lives that were shaped by men. Without telling too much of her business, my mom didn't have an easy life before she met my dad, and then her life was impacted by his addiction, and then hers as well, in ways I can't understand. I didn't want to be judgmental about that, even though my real-life self can be at times. I don't think that any of this pain is good for anyone. Maybe the end is about choosing escape, but really, it's about not knowing what to do next.

Speaking of what to do next, I'm always thinking about "next books." So many people I know write their first book over a long period of time (throughout college and their 20s, for instance), then their second and subsequent books become more intentionally themed and curated. Did you have this experience here? How do you suggest other poets might approach that second (or third or fourth) book? How will you approach your next one?

In a way I did write my first book over a long period of time as you say, and then this one came together in a few years. I did kind of fall into the subject though, because my dad died suddenly. I researched and read a lot of other books that informed my thinking on writing about grief. In this way it has been a more themed and curated experience.

With my next project, I'm thinking about love and relationships. I'm really deliberately trying to write a series of love poems to my husband, to past loves, to girlhood friends, to my parents and my siblings, and even to myself. It's been a process to move out of some of the themes that I've been working with, but if I still want to write about girlhood, I just let myself do it and then go back to trying to write love poems.

Would you like to share any of those books that informed your writing on grief? What's the best way to approach writing through something so heavy?

I don't know the best way to approach writing about something so heavy, but I tried to do it by being imaginative. I mean, I have a poem about a real ghost in a fake haunted house in the same book where I write about my dad siphoning gas from neighborhood cars. It wanted this to be a back and forth between memory and imagination. To name just a couple of books, Diana Khoi Nguyen's *Ghost Of* and Cynthia Cruz's *How the End Begins* are two that I come back to a lot. *Ghost of* is a book about the poet's brother who committed suicide. The use of cesura and cut out language in that book creates a ghostly effect that is very powerful. *How the End Begins* has a similar theme, among other themes, and has a kind of recurring effect, as the themes and images repeat throughout the book. Also, Cruz has a dark and moody way of writing that I love.

In some ways, this book does feel like a love poem. There is a lot of love here in the act of grief. To look back on this book and forward into the next, what do you think makes a good love poem?

That is what I'm trying to figure out now. I do think there is a lot of love in both of my books. I love my parents, but there has been a lot of trauma between us. I love the places where I grew up, but again, the memory is mixed with pain. It's kind of funny because every time I try to write a "love poem" for my husband, it always comes out a reflection on his (or our) mortality. Maybe for me that is love. It's cherishing someone because of that ultimate end.

ACKNOWLEDGEMENTS

First, thank you to *Driftwood Press* for believing in my work. I would also like to thank some wonderful people who helped me along the journey of writing this manuscript. Thank you to Becca Klaver and Dan Rzicznek for reading and commenting on early versions of the book. Thank you to my fellow PhD and MFA students at Georgia State (Especially Karen Javits). Thank you to all my mentors over the years, but a special thank you to Beth Gylys and Danielle Cadena Deulen who helped shape this manuscript. Finally, thank you to my family (All Snyders, Carlyles, Pavlideses, Kales, and Doolittles.)! I love you all. Thank you for your support. I want to especially thank my husband Shane for championing everything I do, and just being a fun guy, and thank you to my cats Sara and Frank and my silly little Dog, Dorothy. You didn't do anything to help with the manuscript, but you are all very cute.

Many thanks to the following journals and magazines where these poems first appeared, some in slightly different forms or different titles:

"Transformation," *Common Ground Review*, 2024
"Opioid Crisis," *Midway Journal*, 2024
"Black Peaches," *American Literary Review*, 2023
"Every House I Ever Lived in as a Child," *Flint Hills Review*, 2023
"I saw a news story: three young girls, shoplifters, caught," *pamplmousse*, 2023
"Cat Guide," *pamplmousse*, 2023
"My Father Siphons Gas," *Stoneboat Literary Journal*, 2023
"A Dream After Watching Stalker During Fire Season," *Harpur Palate*, 2023
"Are We Really Living in a Simulation," *Arts and Letters*, 2023
"21 Years Later," *Haunted Anthology, Porkbelly Press*, 2023
"Yes, No, Goodbye," *Haunted Anthology , Porkbelly Press*, 2023
"Airspace," *Stoneboat Literary Journal*, 2022
"End of the World (I'm sitting at a bus stop, waiting)," *Jet Fuel*, 2022
"Daddy Dream Suite," *Barnstorm Journal*, 2022
"Trying to Communicate," *The Gingerbread House*, 2022
"Moon Landing," *Five South*, 2021
"A Brief History," *Tupelo Quarterly*, 2021
"Things We Believe as Children," *On the Seawall*, 2021
"Just a Village Girl," *The Black Fox Review*, 2021

Photography: Shane Snyder

Erin Carlyle is a poet and educator from Alabama and Kentucky. Her poetry often deals with the intersections of place, poverty, and girlhood. While poetry is her first love, she also enjoys film and music, and is an avid record collector. She lives in Atlanta, Georgia with her husband, two cats, and one dog.

OTHER DRIFTWOOD PRESS TITLES

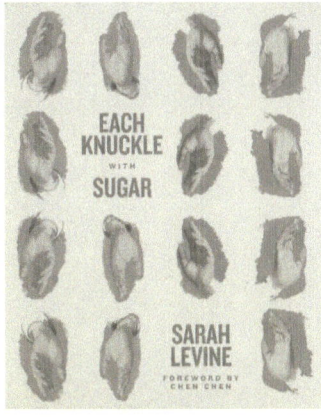

www.ingramcontent.com/pod-product-compliance
Lightning Source LLC
Chambersburg PA
CBHW060537080526
44586CB00012B/776